Toni's Room

A poetic journey to restoration

M. Tonita Austin

(a.k.a Toni Love)

Secretaire

Giving honor and blessings for the love and guidance of my ancestors and angels : my mother Ethelyne Vaughn-Connor, my first teacher who taught me to read before I was old enough to attend school; my father Jabez Thomas Austin Jr. an incredible yet unpublished writer; my third grade teacher Mrs. Tolliver for encouraging me to continue writing poetry; my professor Amiri Baraka for introducing me to black women writer; Ntozake Shange for her profound influence, my grandfather Jabez Thomas Austin for the gift of passionate oration and MaryBelle Austin my constant angel and namesake.

I bless and thank every host of every poetry venue for providing the space for artists like myself to share their love for the written word. I love and bless Sonia Sanchez for my first experience reciting poetry before a crowd, Ursula Rucker for unknowingly giving me permission to embrace the performance poet in myself, my brothers Jay, Jerome and Joel and my dear friends who always show up to support my readings and every single person blessing me with their purchase of this book.

This poetry book is a promise I made to myself years ago after I published my poetry CD. I wanted to embrace more than the hopeless romantic within me. Toni's Room allows the reader deeper into various corners of my soul. My poems expose my honest journey as a black woman to healing through grief, heartbreak, generational trauma, social injustice and solo parenting within the comfort of art and self love. Come on in to Toni's Room. I hope you stay a while.

~ Toni Love

Contents

Title Page
Secretaire
Dedication
Born of Warriors 1
For My Teacher 5
Can't Get You Out of My Head 10
Creation 12
Finally Over 14
Grief Waits 16
I Remember You (For Mommy) 20
I Surrender 23
I Want to Be Your Addiction 25
I Remember You (or Basement duet for Queen B) 27
I Want To Get Off 31
Kwanzaa 34
Old School Love 36
Lost 39
Not One (For the Million Mothers March Oct 2016) 40
Saxophone Solo 43
Tanka 1 (Praying) 47

Tanka 2 (Fallen)	48
Purple Haiku for You	49
We Are Here (Welcome Home)	50
The Day I Left God	55
Shades - The Prelude	60
#WCW	61
Haiku for my soul (Some days are real hard)	63
The Restoration	64

"Perhaps everybody has a garden of Eden, I don't know; but they have scarcely seen their garden before they see the flaming sword. Then, perhaps, life only offers the choice of remembering the garden or forgetting it. Either, or: it takes strength to remember, it takes another kind of strength to forget, it takes a hero to do both."

— JAMES BALDWIN, GIOVANNI'S ROOM

This book of poetry is dedicated to my two greatest creations, my children James and Janai who gave up a bit of me so I could finish this project. Mommy loves you so. Thank you.

Born of Warriors

Now is not the time to sit down and grow weary

For we are born of warriors

Trained on soil rich with the spirits that passed before us

We were selected from our tribe and trained for battle

Even stripped of our land, our riches and our families

We stood strong ushering the chained weary in front of us

Walking miles to the beach to meet our battle with the sea

Some were not strong enough to endure the nausea swaying beneath our ribs

Diseased corpses laying by, vicious attacks of salt water on open wounds

Watching the constant raping of wombs and deep screams of torment

Many were not trained for this battle and vanished into the sea at night for comfort

They were not capable of taking the journey so they took their

Mary Tonita Austin

own lives instead

    But we did not

We are born of warriors

We were trained for this

Taught how to survive capture

How to lead without authority

Torment and torture we withstood

       We are born of warriors

So this is nothing new

We will always come up against those who never wish to see us free

They have seen us rule, prosper and conquer

They seek to degrade, demoralize and destroy our power

We have forgotten who we are

    But they have not

They fear us because we are born of warriors

Now is not the time to be paralyzed in fear

Queens expect their sons to walk off into battle

Tears rolling down the backs of their Kings as they prepare sons for their destiny

Never is the battle fair

Never is the outcome expected

But we must not sit and fight battles with feathers
Now is the time to stand up and fight

    Remember who you are

Your ancestors did not fall weak and die before reaching land

Nor did they jump to their demise

They stood and fought and ran and rallied and walked and planned and waited and revolted but they did not sit down

The only reason you are here is because they fought for your life

Never forget that some will never cease at trying to capture your freedom

You were born for this

You were trained for the battle

You are here solely because you are born of warriors

Those who seek to destroy you have not forgotten
You descended from Kings and Queens

Mary Tonita Austin

Born a warrior

For My Teacher
a thank you letter to Amiri Baraka

Unexpected the tears i feel

crawling up my throat

pushing aside my sensibilities

why?

you were just my teacher

others have hours upon lifetimes

of close contact and deep ties

experiences transcendetal with you

you were just my teacher

teacher

black man

scholar

activist

Mary Tonita Austin

poet

playwrite

king

presence

present

gifted

presence

it was your presence

strolling across the white washed campus

ivy league columns seemed to part as you

floated down the pyramid-esque stairs

making way to your classroom

my father we saw often as he waved goodbye and walked out the door

working at night while we slept

sleeping during the day as we crept

around trying not to make a sound

trying not to be too loud

trying to love breathe and be without him knowing we were even around

surfacing after a Jack Daniels induced slumber

yelling for his crisp white t shirt iron warm

button down and jeans with pressed creases

my father taught me that men treasured work not love

mother taught me how to exist within the needs of another

amiri baraka taught me about presence

missing the presence of black women writers in the libraries of west philadelphia schools

i stumbled upon Lorraine Hansberry in boarding school

stuck between shakespeare and uncle tom's cabin while searching for reflections of me

my white male librarian ordered a peek into this phenomenal writer that looked like me

my teacher widened my view

sitting in the front of the class

ready to inhale every word

watching his facila expressions

waiting for him to notice my existence

Mary Tonita Austin

in awe of every sight of you

educated, passionate, musical, angry, gifted, activist black man like my father

you tought me much more than words

it was within that time and space i fell in love with Ntozake Shange, Alice Walker, Nikki Giovanni, Sonia Sanchez, Gwendolyn Brooks, Toni Morrison and Angela Davis

it was then

it was them

it was you

it was your presence that taught me the power of my existence

you were my teacher

my experience lasted beyond your stroll out of the classroom off campus and onto the #2

it is your presence

your presence i miss

strong black man

confident black man

unapologetic black man

father figure

Toni's Room

in so many ways

you were my teacher

Can't Get You Out of My Head

your voice slides inside my mind like silk panties between my thighs

and i can't get you out of my head

so sweet and so unique i could listen to your sexiness until i fell off to sleep

for now i'll just imagine you laying your body across my bed

yearning to feel your touch your lips and waiting for the first passionate kiss

i can't believe i'm capable of feeling like this

have i finally met my match, a romantic whose words are as sweet as a hershey's kiss

or my soul mate able to touch me so deeply that i can't resist

your eyes and your smile leave me yearning for your loving caress

imagining you and i hand in hand heart to heart

makes me feel warm and sticky like honey dripping down the back of my dress

i want you, you want me and we both find ourselves weak from the thought

of opening up our souls and hearts as they intertwine into an eternal rope of passion and ecstasy

you make love to my mind and i can't say no

i surrender all

you are my destiny

just lay my body down on your lavender scented bed

cause i can't get you out of my head.

Creation

Look at me
I am creativity
I created the stars in your eyes
I created the warmth in these skies
It is I who is worldly and wise
It is I who you see in the beauty of the butterflies.

I am the artist and the dancer
The center of all creation
When I reveal myself
There is no limitation.

I can soar across the globe
  by extending my hands
I can travel among all space/all time
Just as the insect travels among the sands
      I am creativity.
I am the writer and the poet
I can touch all of humanity
With the motion of my pen.

I can capture your soul with mere words

And you wouldn't even know it

Until I finished.

Until the end.

For I am truth

love

beauty

   and sin.

Look at me

I am creativity

I am your inner destiny

But I have no end.

Finally Over

when i lost you

i found myself

oh but it hurt

it pained for so long

thinking of how foolish i had been

to believe in you

but my hurt turned into poetry

and dance

and i wrote

and danced

until i filled up the emptiness in side of me

the void that set inside my soul when you were no longer there poetry about you and for myself

flowed from my fingertips like golden run at carnival time in trinidad

i loved until i stopped hurting

and found not only myself
but someone to love me for real

oh yes i admit there were times i wished that he were you

until constant caresses and truthful sighs

showed me that true love accepts me for what i am

oh yes

    it is finally over

real love has rescued my weary soul

and you are but a faded memory

because i am no longer afraid to receive the love

that i have been given

Grief Waits

she cries

into makeup stained pillows when no one is awake

this single mother of two wants her own daddy   back

but no time to be sad with taxi runs to baseball ballet and

piano lessons

no chance to cry with the babies watching and counting on

her strength

even peaceful meditation is interrupted by children's night-

mares soaked in sadness

she greets the morning sun holding back the tears

adorning sunglasses so the suburban moms don't ask her

"what's wrong?" as she skips her child to school

gotta make sure her offspring are happy and

gotta make sure they keep up their grades and

gotta keep their schedules full of activities so they won't feel the pain

gotta keep a smile at the job and

gotta search for the desire to pay the bills, do the laundry and cook a healthy meal

gotta shield them from the rain

but who is taking care of the little girl who just lost her daddy

who makes sure she eats and

keeps the

heaviness of her heart from sinking into the pit of her stomach

who holds back her fear of raising black children alone while the village is slowly disappearing

no grandfathers, no grandmothers, great grands, no mother /no father

Mary Tonita Austin

no father

who holds her at the end of the night when the kids are counting sheep and she can't find enough energy to weep

who takes her by the hand and lifts her off her feet to give her burdens a chance to sleep

who says its gonna be okay and wipes her tears away

maybe tomorrow will be a better day

maybe then she'll feel like going out to play

but not today

because she's tossed and turned all night

living a nightmare until the first ray of daylight

then its time to dab away the pain and push away the tears

because its 7:15 and the school bus will soon be here

and no one wants salty tears in their lunchbox

weary, she rises once again meeting the morning with a smile

as grief waits behind every closed door

god bless the child

I Remember You (*For Mommy*)

With every embrace

I remember you

In every poem I write

I honor you

Each boo-boo I kiss

Every time I drop everything to respond to a call from the school

I invoke glimpses of your face

I remember you

Prayers tucked into soft wrinkles of your hand

Wisdom in the tight grey coils that framed a crown of compassion on your forehead

Baby oil in the bathtub and Vaseline on your feet

Callouses from walking your journey with no shoes

Allowing the earth as a cushion beneath

Fourteen years, 5,110 days, 112640 hours and 7,358,400 minutes

The time lapse does not stop tears and memories from flooding my heart

I remember you

Homemade cigarettes in the basement

Not knowing you found comfort exhaling

You inhaled concoctions of joy, sadness, loss and grief both liberating and toxic

I speak of you to your grandchildren

Chance meetings as souls passed in transition

They remember you though never met you here on earth

I hear you in the deep vibrato of Nina Simone and Lou Rawls

I smell you in the cinnamon nutmeg infused sweet potato pie I can't quite get to taste the same

I see you in the eyes of my son you ushered onto this plane

Mary Tonita Austin

My children speak of past lives with you

I cry for you

I laugh with you

I speak to you

I still need you

I wait to hear you

I call and you still answer

I remember you

And thank you

For remembering me too

I Surrender

Been tossing and turning all night
just as my weary eyelids begin to close
they reflect scenes of you and I struggling
through our first fight
My mind replays the who what when and why
my head tells my heart not to break down and cry
cause it doesn't understand how it can love you
and ache to hate you at the same time
I want to stay angry
so I scan my memories for reasons to leave you
to ignore you, to believe you
The more we talk the more I see
how important communication is to strengthen
the bond between you and me
for it dissolves the mounds of fear built up over the years
from the deceit of those who could not love me

I want to stay angry convincing myself it's easier to be alone than in love

But you love me unconditionally and refuse to leave me be
A moment of weakness and you climb my wall
I finally take your call
Intentionally sending through words that
you know will melt my heart
not to mention my other body parts
The next thing I know you're at my door
and we're holding each other
with promises and whispers of forgiveness
as our clothes hit the floor
Our lips meet and I forget what all that arguing was for
We come together and become one
As I surrender

I Want to Be Your Addiction

i want to be your addiction

i want you to dream of me
wake up thinking of me
can't wait to touch skin with me
yearning for me to take you to ecstasy
hold me and desire me
inhale me absorb me savor every drop of me
fold me into your physique like my dress folds into my inner thigh

i want to be your addiction

i want to possess your mind
flow through every curvature of your body
make you want to get up out of your warm bed at night just to have me
full body sweat and fever when you desire the dope of me to be within you

Mary Tonita Austin

i want to be your addiction

i want you to need me

to breathe me

to spend your last dime just to fill your atmosphere with me

i want to take you higher

make your heart sing

change the neurons in your mind

make you lose track of time

i want to be your addiction

i want you to be a fiend for me

want you to concede that i am all that you need

i want

/ to be/

 your/

addiction

I Remember You (*or Basement duet for Queen B*)

We sang into West Philly-bred microphones

Scents of stale beer and cigarettes floating under our basement borne concerts

Roberta Flack

Natalie Cole

Teena Marie

They were us we were we and we were free

Imagining concert halls filled with fans gasping for gardenia scented motions of us

We danced swaying under water pipes and wooden rafters

Dressed in summer swag, tossing braids and permed ponytails while we bumped hips and dipped knees

We were stars on the dust filled unfinished basement stage

Mary Tonita Austin

    It was all we knew

We were inseparable until you strayed

We went our separate ways

You succumbed to painful nights soaked in old men calling for you to dance again

Dark midnight alley romance offering snow dust dreams and green smoke behind masks

You danced to stale music with no voice

Now you're gone and with you our Webster street duet

Yet

I still hear you

We walk together in a parallel universe

Pushing my stroller under the suburban sunshine

I think of my sister pushing through the door at the crack of dawn

Both rising to meet our children

Both trying to define success in the way we could see

Yet

I still see you

Walking alone waiting on the bus stop in clothes wrinkled in the scent of cigars and whiskey

As I secure the seat belt of my luxury car at the corner of my single home

We both sit cloaked in sadness

I walk with you though you don't see my journey

Resting in the sorrow of acceptance that I could not save you from yours

I remember you

I see you

I carry you

I sing for you

I write for you

I swing my hips for you

Mary Tonita Austin

I inhale smoke filled rooms and sip beer through a straw for you

I plant my feet and grab the mic in remembrance of you

You support me

I carry you

I love you

I remember you

I miss you

I will always

REMEMBER

YOU

I Want To Get Off

i approach you carefully hesitating all the while

feeling my body being pulled closer because you entice

me and i love your style

so sexy the way you dip when you move

silky smooth colored outer skin and your softness in-

side makes me want to sink in to you

no doubt so many fall in line just to be in your presence

here i am among them unashamed waiting for my turn

to experience the same

ecstasy

i stand patiently with my heart quickly racing

thousands of beats per minute fill my heaving chest

as you motion in my direction

Mary Tonita Austin

my body temperature elevates my palms are moist
waiting to feel you inside
breathing heavily, approaching cautiously til you pull me close and wrap yourself around my waist and outer thigh

i hold you tight and close my eyes
too afraid to just let go and enjoy the ride

i trust the way you ease into it gently and take it slow
the excitement builds and my heart sinks down to my feet and i forget how really fast we are going

and just when my climax begins
you drop me
and leave me
helpless

no air to breathe, no support under my feet and i don't feel the passion anymore

i'm scared and i don't know what's coming next

i can't trust that you are secure enough to protect me

even holding me as tight as you can, i still scream from fear

i'm afraid that when i trust you the most you'll unloose me

so i beg you to stop playing with my heart
to unwrap yourself from my torso and release me
let me walk away with my dignity, without feeling ashamed about what i let you do to me

i foolishly trusted you from the start and now that you've shaken both my confidence and my heart

you will never convince me again to ride a roller coaster

i'll stick to the kiddie go-carts!

Kwanzaa

Black colors

Brown faces

Strong arms to hold and embrace you

Big smiles

Hearty laughter

Habari Gani

Smells of ancestors lurking in each corner of the house

Rising from the love scented crumpled foil

Floating in on recipes passed down through generations

Warm pots and pans carried in the hands of family

Friends who cherish our rituals and faith

Stand by to learn

To share

Umoja

Children laughing, playing

Yearning to participate

Warm Sahara colored food on their plates

Love

Warmth

Family

Ancestors

Kwanzaa

Old School Love

i'm yearnin' for some old school love
that sweet love that kept you up on the phone all night
not thinking of short verses for his twitter page but
$$\begin{aligned}&\text{long}\\&\text{drawn}\\&\text{out}\\&\text{sighs}\end{aligned}$$

movement from lip to thighs
sweet nothings to fill your ear and make you want to
dis appear

into the abyss of his love

into the phone for a sloppy kiss and a tight hug

not pictures of his body on facebook or pictures that some
                              other body
took
but cuddling up next to each other on the couch
not texting each other but
hand to hand
mouth to mouth

can't wait to wrap up inside of that warm oven kind of love
that sweet love when he would rush home after work
to take you for a walk around the park

write your name up in the sky and tell you

you're the reason why

you wanting to be his lover girl
praying he'd take you for a trip around the world
or even just a push on a swing
and one day a shiny diamond ring

both
wishing on a star
that no one would see you in the backseat of that car
vowing to love each other
       for-e-ver
as you sunk deep into that leather

i want that old school love

i want his hand to slowly caress my back
not the touch screen of his phone
i want us to feel like we're all alone

not with a zillion other friends chatting, messaging and interrupting

when he puts my face in his hands and says that this is where he wants to be
the only tweeting that i want to hear is sweet nothing whispered in my ear
or music playing softly as he lay near

and though i know that things are different

in this time and age

Mary Tonita Austin

and that most people and relationships are not much more than comments thrown all around the page but

i want that

old
school
love

i know you're out there

and until you find your way through

i'll be saving all my love / saving all my love/
saving all my love for you

Lost

My heart is lost in a place

My head tried so desperately

To keep it from wandering

Not One (*For the Million Mothers March Oct 2016*)

Not mine son

Not mine

Not my son

Not my brother nephew or current lover

Not my neighbor cousin or future husband

Not mine

Not hers

Not anybody's

Son

I am not saying no more

I am saying not ONE

We with the millions of ancestors behind us

Forge a force you will feel into centuries

Your generations will not be safe

Your land will not be prosperous

Your wealth will not sustain you

Your privilege will not save you

We are millions today plus millions before u

Far more than your eyes can see

We gather together seen and unseen

When mothers pray it goes straight to heaven

Rest assured and be forewarned

There will be a price for your descendants to pay

If you ever look at my son in a disrespectful, condescending or threatening way

Mary Tonita Austin

We collectively are not playing with you today

No more

Not one

Not

One

More

Son

Saxophone Solo

And just who do you think you are that you could build up my emotions

strong as the ancient egyptian pyramids

only to leave them scattered

like the crumbs at the bottom of grandma's cookie

jar after the sweet treats are gone

And who are you that you could sweet talk me

into giving up myself once closed

Pure as Georgia sugar cane and just as sweet

Giving up my sweet sugar like the saxophone

gives into the soft touch of lips

and fingertips

of Grover

or Coltrane

Giving in

hoping that what comes from the sacrifice will be everlasting

    But you played me for only a 3-count phrase and laid
        me down to free your hands for another
        and I am left to do a solo performance with
            no assistance from you.
    And I thought since making musical love waz your
      thing that what I had inside was enough for you
        but my dance and my poems and sensuous soul
          filled with rhapsodies and roses
          no none of that was enough

    You were like all men arrogant enough to look for
        whatever wasn't coming your way
        And what you found had to be beautiful with long permed hair

      and she had to have that money

green as the grass we parted when we were once lovers

Yes your new love had to be full of those superficial qualities that satisfy your black bourgeois mentality

No deep sister who knew black men and could
tell you more about Farrakhan or Medgar Evers
then they themselves knew

No real woman whose hair went nappy when wet
with water from midnight showers

with big feet, healthy thighs and common sense

But since you're one of those so-called men who haven't
yet recognized the unique essence of a true black woman
you can keep your lips and fingers to yourself

For I'd rather cry for my sisters in Soweto march
for my brother Trayvon and fast for

my people in the Sudan before I ever

Ever

let your lips playing games of kiss and lie and your
fingers boasting empty caresses touch my soul

again

in life.

Mary Tonita Austin

                Because I am no fool

and

            Just who do you think I am

                  anyway?

Tanka 1 (*Praying*)

tight hugs and laughter

if only i knew one day

they'd both drift away

too soon and with her i'd lay

praying for a miracle

Tanka 2 (*Fallen*)

caught up so sweetly

a prisoner of my fear

now sleep escapes me

i have fallen so deeply

in love that i cannot breathe

Purple Haiku for You

when doves cry tears fall

wet from passion in hues of you

love is the answer

We Are Here (*Welcome Home*)

Grey birds whisper through the trees

Ancestors swaying the leaves

calling my name in threes

To-nee-tah!

Toni!

Niiiiii-taaaah

We are HERE

WE are here

We ARE here

and so should you be

here

present

listening

walking

breathing

feeling

touching

writing

connecting with us

we have wisdom to speak into you

Mary Tonita Austin

those chirps ARE a call to action

the leaves of soft swaying trees beckon
you to come near

those ARE drums in the distance

We are the Lenape the Massai and the Blackfoot

The soil beneath your feet is moist to
comfort your journey

we are you

you are we

we are here

When you are here the sun beams and clouds
part celebrating your presence

this feels like home because you are home

Yemeya we call you

Oshun misses you

There is peace here

Come

Sit

Hear

Embrace

Inhale

Exhale

It is safe here

This is no coincidence

Mary Tonita Austin

We have called you and you listened

Never forget us

Stay open

We need you to tell our stories

If you take the time to listen

we will always welcome you home

Although you may leave

we do not

we / are / here

The Day I Left God

i laid the red carnation on top of her casket

collapsing through showers of grief

the sight of them lowering the flesh and bones of my mother into the cold hard ground was too much

for my fragile womb to bear

i prophesized years before

that her life would end when her decayed lungs could take no more

tobacco

stress

worry

fear

yet i still was not prepared

god was not supposed to take my mommy so soon

Mary Tonita Austin

i did all the right things

i was baptized and attended church

i paid my tithes

helped the elderly, sick and poor

volunteered and served my community

graduated from college, supported myself

and although i wasn't perfect i tried to do

every righteous thing i could do

stayed by her side like a good daughter should

took her to doctor's appointments

brought her clothes and food when she was unable to move

i was so good

how could he take my mommy so soon?

every day i walked into the cancer center i stopped by the chapel to pray please wait until my baby is born before you take my mommy away

every day

on my knees i would pray

please god

please god

and he took her anyway

standing over her casket tears flowing too fast to even wipe away

i sobbed again for her grandbaby comfortably swaying in my womb

anxious to see the light of day

not realizing the would never get the chance to wrap his little

hands around her face and say

   i love you mom mom

day by day the anger filled up every space left in my perforated heart

how dare my god leave me to do motherhood alone?

without my mother to tell me how to hold him when to feed him

when to worry and when to let go

how cruel can he be to leave me mourning during the most beautiful time in my life?

just two months before i would walk down the aisle and become someone's loving wife

with each contraction my unborn child had no choice but to drink in my tears of pain grief and anger

my soul cried out

>   *Whyyyyyyyyyyy*

and received no answer

i found myself sitting in silence once again

praying to find the strength to go on

so i did what i felt god had done

i banished love and left my soul deserted

back in the cemetery in the cold hard earth i left my faith in god and buried it deep

and i walked away

and i wept

the day i left god

Shades - The Prelude

There was once a time

I thought the sun would never

Warm my face again

Until you pushed back

My heart's cloud with fierce passion

Letting the light in

#WCW

can i be your woman crush wednesday

will you put me on your feed

on those cold and lonely mornings before you turn on your tv

will you wonder what i'm doing

find your way onto my page

scrolling through my profile pictures

imagining yourself the subject of my gaze

thinking we could have those moments

holding me close under your sheet

wishing you could be the recipient of the sexy smile that makes you weak

can i be your woman crush wednesday
post me up and love me true

Mary Tonita Austin

if you stroke my ego today

monday i'll be sure to stroke yours too

would you?

Haiku for my soul (*Some days are real hard*)

many days i cry in deep

crevices of my pillow

praying the ghosts of past loved

ones will appear / swaddling me with comfort

yet i wait

The Restoration

i sat in the sun and felt mother earth
unwrap the cloak of stress and strain from around my shoulders

she said

> *you are a healer*

> *you now know this to be true*

> *your children needed the restoration*

> *only you could provide*

> *i have heard your midnight cries*

> *i have answered your prayers*

> *it is now time to heal yourself*

> *it is time*

i stepped forward into the sun to accept her will for me

Toni's Room

Yes

i answered

It Is Time

Copyright © 2019 by Toni Love Publishing
Media, PA 19063

All rights reserved. No part of this book may be reproduced, stored in a retrieval system, or transmitted in any form or by any means electronic, mechanical, photocopying, recording or otherwise, used in any manner without written permission of the copyright owner except for the use of quotations in a book review.

Cover design by M. Tonita Austin

Cover photography by Lynece Austin of Austin Fine Photography

For more information, contact Mary Tonita Austin by email: tonitalove2@gmail.com

FIRST EDITION

www.tonitalove.com

For engagements: www.marytonitaaustin.com